THE PRINCE OF EGYPT

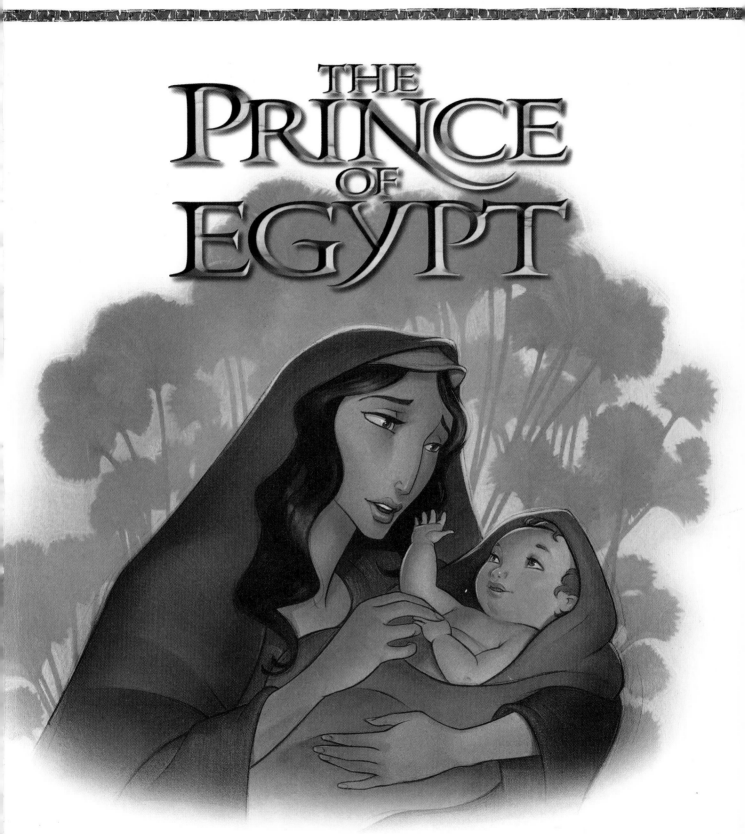

Adapted by Jane Yolen
Painted by Michael Köelsch

Penciled by Larry Navarro

DreamWorks.

Once the Hebrew people lived happily in the land of the Nile. They dwelt side by side with the Egyptians, working with them, their children playing together under the shelter of the palms.

But when a new Pharaoh came to the throne of Egypt, he felt that the Hebrews had grown too numerous, strong, and mighty. He even feared they might turn against his own Egyptian people. So he set the Egyptians as masters over them.

Listen, my children, to the story of Moses, who was once a prince of Egypt but became something far greater. It is a story of faith and deliverance. It is a story of freedom.

Mud, sand, water, straw to make bricks, and the sharp sting of the overseer's whip—that was the lot of the Hebrew slaves in Egypt. Hundreds died under the lash. Hundreds more of the heavy burden of work.

But Pharaoh feared the Hebrews were still too many.

"Throw all the newborn Hebrew boys into the Nile!" he ordered. "Let the crocodiles feast."

Now one woman gave birth to a baby boy just after this order was sent throughout the land. So she hid the infant for three months while her daughter Miriam and her older son, Aaron, brought her all she needed.

But at last she knew the child could not be kept safe as long as he was with her.

"The Lord will protect and keep you," she whispered to him. And then she sang a lullaby full of promises and prayers. *"Be still, love, don't cry,"* she sang. *"I will be with you when you dream."*

She made a basket of bulrushes, daubing it with pitch so that it would be watertight. Tenderly, she placed the baby in it and put the cover on top. Then, weeping, she set the basket on the River Nile.

The river rocked the child to sleep and awake again. And so sleeping and waking, he was carried past crocodiles swimming, past hippopotamuses wallowing, past boatmen fishing, past soldiers marching, past mile upon mile until the basket fetched up at last on a quiet shore.

All this young Miriam had seen as she spied on the basket's perilous journey.

And she saw it come to rest in the water garden of the queen of Egypt, who was there with her handmaidens and her young son Rameses. When the basket was deposited by the river at her feet, the queen lifted the cover and saw the infant smiling up at her.

She knew it was a Hebrew child, but she did not care. She saw only the sweet face, the dark eyes, the innocent hand reaching up to her. She believed that the child in the basket had surely been kept safe by the gods of Egypt especially for her, for she had always wanted another son.

So the queen picked up the baby and named him Moses, which means "drawn out," for she had drawn him out of the water.

Turning to her own firstborn, the queen said, "Come, Rameses. We will show Pharaoh your new baby brother."

For many years Moses lived as a pampered son of the Pharaoh. He did not know that he was really the son of slaves. Indeed, he did not think about the slaves at all, any more than he thought about the bricks upon which the kingdom of Egypt was built. Bricks made of water, mud, straw, and the blood of the Hebrew people.

With his brother Rameses, Moses raced through life with little care for the people beneath him. He was young and strong and full of vigor. He was a prince. A prince of Egypt.

The Pharaoh often reprimanded his boisterous sons. He would remind them that a kingdom could not be built on excess. He told them that the rulers of a kingdom must never be reckless and destructive.

"When I pass into the Next World," he would say, "then you, Rameses, will be the morning and the evening star. Be careful what you do. One weak link can break the chain of a mighty empire."

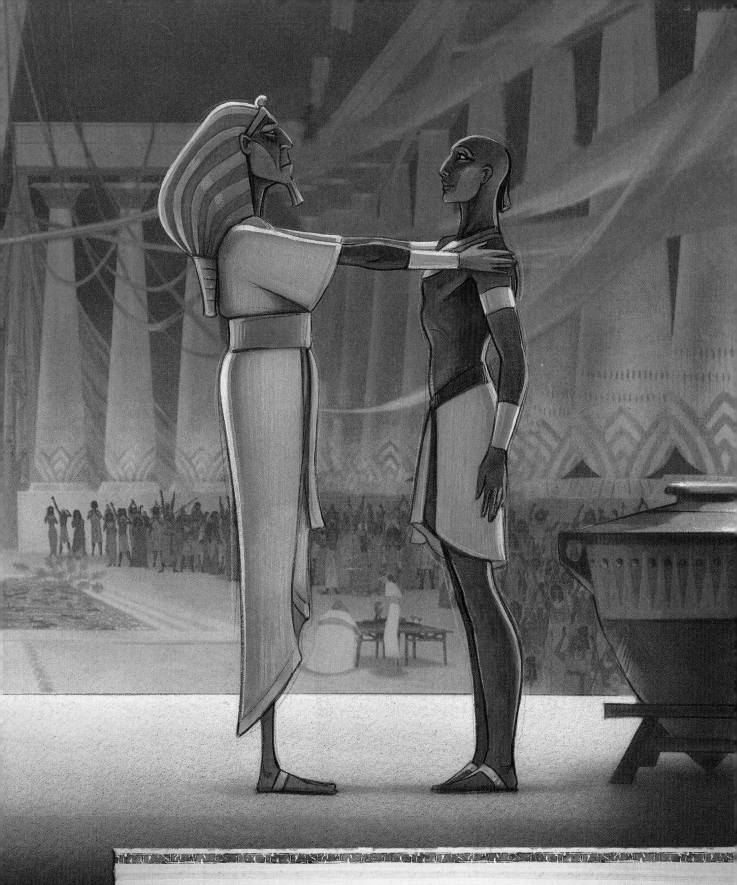

Moses was only the second son after all, and he knew that he would never rule Egypt, but he loved his brother Rameses well. He suggested to Pharaoh that Rameses only needed the opportunity to show their father the strength that was in his heart. So when the queen told them that Rameses was to be given greater responsibilities in the kingdom as a test of that strength, Moses rejoiced.

In return, his brother appointed Moses chief architect of the rebuilding of some of the temples. And he gave Moses a present: a girl stolen from the Midianites, one of the desert tribes.

Prince to prince, a gift of a slave.

But the girl was full of fire and daring, for the desert had made her strong. Intrigued, Moses distracted the guards and she escaped, racing through the courtyard and through the streets of the great city into Goshen, where the slaves were quartered.

Not knowing why he followed, Moses went after her.

Moses had never actually been in Goshen before, where the great majority of the slaves lived. Goshen had dark, narrow, twisting streets. He found himself lost there and a little bit afraid.

A prince of Egypt afraid?

It could not be so. So he did not let it be.

One last dark turning, and he saw ahead several slaves standing and chatting by a well, so he pulled back into the shadows to watch for a moment. But when at last he came forward and revealed himself, one of the slaves—a dark-eyed, black-haired young woman—was so startled she dropped a clay water pot.

"To see you here...at our door...at last, Brother," she cried.

Moses had come, all unknowing, to the very place where his brother Aaron and sister Miriam lived—Miriam, the one who had watched as the basket had carried baby Moses to the feet of Egypt's queen.

"Brother!" she cried again, for though Moses did not know her, she knew him well. "Brother!"

"I am no brother of yours," he said.

Quickly, pleadingly, she told him the story of his journey down the Nile, past the hungry crocodiles and the soldiers with their long spears. She told him that he had been born to deliver his people from Egypt, a land where the Pharaoh ordered the slaughter of baby boys. And when he would not listen, when he turned to go as if disgusted by the nattering of a slave, she began to sing a lullaby, the very lullaby his mother had sung so long ago.

"*Be still, love, don't cry,*" Miriam sang. "*I will be with you when you dream.*"

For a moment Moses remembered, and he felt again the waves rocking him awake and asleep. But only for a moment.

How could he believe her? To believe Miriam meant that his life of grace and pleasure had been built on the back of a lie. To believe her meant that the father he revered, the mother he adored had been untruthful to him. To believe her meant that he was not the son of Egypt but the child of slaves.

So he ran.

He ran and ran until he got back to the palace that was all the home he had ever known, all he had ever wanted: the sweet perfumes of incense, the graceful alabaster rooms, the hieroglyphs about the glory of Egypt spelled out on the walls.

Tired of running, Moses set his back to a column, fell asleep, and began to dream.

In his dream, the hieroglyphs came alive. All that Miriam had said about the killing of the Hebrew babies and the long trip down the Nile in the basket unfolded before his horrified eyes. Moses wept.

And he woke with a start. Taking a torch, he ran from his room and through the palace until he came at last to a vast chamber.

There, written on the walls, was the truth he had never read: blood, straw, mud, and the babies thrown into the teeth of the waiting beasts.

Moses fell to his knees and this time he wept for real.

Just then, Pharaoh entered the room and put his hand on Moses' shoulder.

"Tell me what happened, Father," Moses asked at last.

"The Hebrews grew too numerous. They might have risen against us."

"Tell me you did not do this," Moses said.

"Sometimes for the greater good," his father answered, his voice hollow with authority, "sacrifices must be made."

"Sacrifices?" Moses thought about the babies. He thought about the crocodiles' sharp teeth.

"They were only slaves," Pharaoh said.

Horrified, Moses ran from the chamber and went down to the Nile.
Here he had been cradled, here he had been saved. And here the queen found him.

"So everything I thought, everything I am, is a lie?" Moses asked.

The queen took his face in her hands. "You are our son and we love you."

"Why did you choose me?"

"We did not choose you, Moses. The gods did. When the gods send a
blessing, you do not ask why it was sent."

If she meant it as comfort, it was little enough. But it was all the comfort
that Moses could find.

Though he was only beginning to realize that he was a son of slaves, Moses was still prince of Egypt to everyone else. As a prince, he had duties to perform. One of these was to join his brother at the site of a ruined temple that Rameses was hoping to rebuild.

Rameses looked at the temple and this is what he saw: columns lying broken in heaps, sand drifting to the knees of the mighty statues. And he saw, too, the temple as it could be: white limestone gleaming in the desert sun.

"I will raise this temple anew that throughout time to come men shall gaze upon it and say, 'Great Rameses built this,'" he said, pride in his voice.

But Moses did not see the broken columns, the drifting sand. He did not see the vision of the temple as it would be. For the first time he saw only the slaves who labored there. Their pain was his pain, their blood his blood.

Moses saw further that high on one of the platforms an old slave accidentally spilled a basket of sand. The Egyptian guard lashed the man, his whip rising and falling like the beat of a heart.

In that moment, Moses understood what suffering meant. He cried out to the guard, "Stop! Stop!"

The guard did not hear him, or if he heard, he did not obey.

In a fury Moses raced up the platform and leaped toward the guard. The guard stumbled and fell down and down and down to the stone floor while Moses, horrified, could only watch.

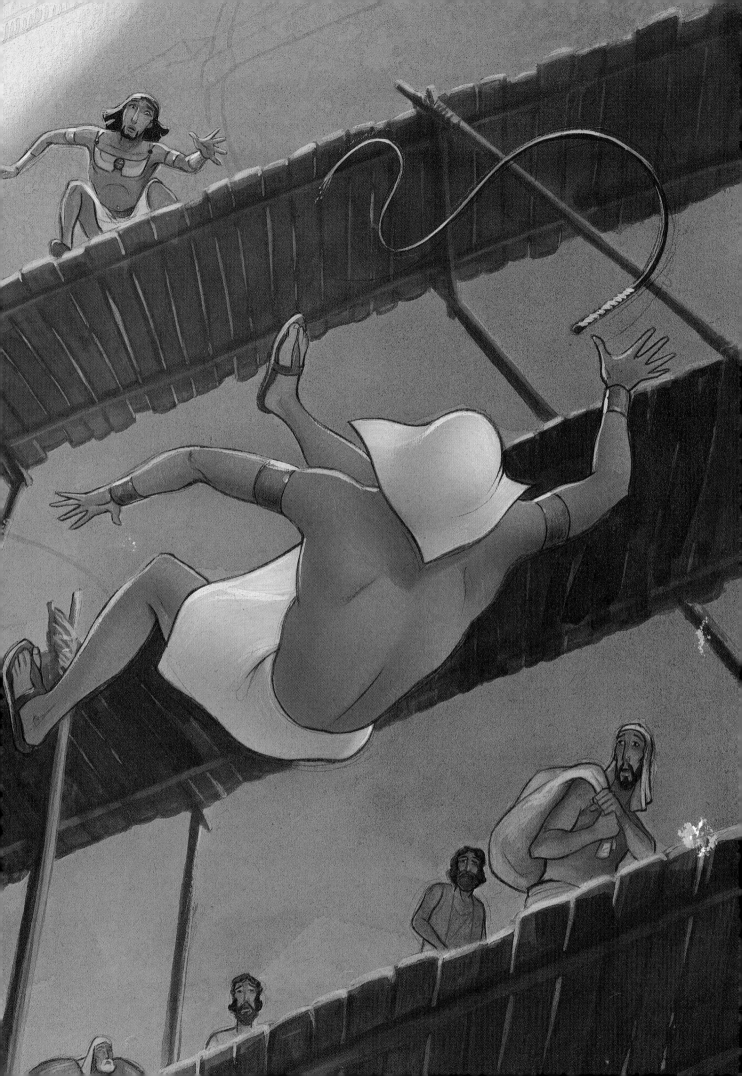

MOSES came down off the platform and stared at the dead guard. His fury left him then, and he was afraid. He had killed a man—and he was afraid.

Rameses put his arm around Moses. "I will make it so it never happened, Brother. If I say day is night, it will be written."

Moses shook his head. "Nothing you say can change what I have done."

The word *nothing* echoed in his head. *Nothing*. Not the love of a mother who had drawn him from the river, not the love of a father who had taught him how to be strong, not the love of a brother who had been his companion in all things.

So Moses fled.

He fled into the vast desert where he was prince no more.

Many days and many nights Moses wandered in the desert. He had nothing to eat, nothing to drink.

The sands scoured his body and face until all that was Egypt was lost to him.

Time went by, measured in grains of sand, until Moses at last stumbled into a village and fetched up against a well.

The first time he almost died, he had been drawn out of water. This time he had been drawn out of sand. He plunged himself into the life-giving water.

No sooner had he taken his first swallow than he heard a nearby shout. A child's cry.

"Help!"

Moses had left Egypt because he could no longer live a lie, because he had killed a man, and because he had learned of the slaughter of babies. Could he remain still now when a child—even a stranger's child—called for help? Struggling to his feet, he heard again the child shouting, though this time she cried: "Leave us alone! Let our flocks drink!"

There were shepherds pushing aside several young girls and their sheep from the well. Moses roused himself and drove the men off. Then exhausted by the effort, he collapsed again by the well.

What a maze of happy accidents. This was the very village that the Midianite girl, Tzipporah, came from. And the children Moses saved from the shepherds who would drive them from the well were the girl's little sisters. And their father, Jethro, was the high priest of Midian.

So there was feasting and dancing.

There was love and laughter.

There was a kind of happy ever after.

For a long while.

Moses stayed with the Midianites, no longer a stranger in a strange land, but a valued member of their tribe. He came to understand that a man's true worth was not measured in palaces and alabaster rooms.

"Learn to look at your life through heaven's eyes," Jethro said, not once but many times.

Moses married the girl Tzipporah and his life became a single bright, straight thread: wife, family, neighbors, friends, and the shepherding of small sheep through the valleys.

If Moses ever thought again about Egypt where he had been a prince, where his sister and brother were still slaves, he did not say. He was happy now in Midian.

But who knows by looking at a single thread what the tapestry itself is like? Who can tell the pattern or make out the design?

If Moses had forgotten Egypt, the Lord God had not, for the Lord's memory is long while man's memory is short. And one day, when Moses was chasing a lost lamb through the wild highlands of the Sinai, by the side of Mount Horeb, he saw an astonishing sight.

Before him was a senna, a thornbush. The bush was burning, its branches bright with flame. Yet as it burned, it was not consumed.

Forgetting the lost lamb, Moses drew nearer. Curious, he put his staff into the bush, then drew it out again. Like the bush, the staff was still whole.

Suddenly a powerful voice spoke from the bush: "Moses!"

"Here I am," replied Moses.

"Take the sandals from off your feet," said the voice from the bush, "for the place where you stand is holy ground."

Moses did so, but all the while he looked down at the ground which was illumined by a strange light. "Who are you?" he asked, trembling.

"I am that I am. I am the God of your ancestors Abraham, Isaac, and Jacob; the God of Sara, Rebecca, Rachel, and Leah."

Afraid, Moses hid his face. "What do you want with me?"

"I have seen the oppression of my people in Egypt and have heard their cry. I shall deliver them out of slavery and bring them to the promised land. So unto Pharaoh I shall send you."

Moses shook. "The Hebrew people will never believe me. I was a prince of Egypt, the son of the man who slaughtered their children. How can *I* speak to them?"

For a moment the voice grew angry. "Who made man's mouth? Did not I?" Then realizing that Moses was afraid, the voice added more softly, "Take the staff in your hand, Moses. With it you shall do my wonders."

Moses raced home and told his wife all that had happened.

"Why you, Moses?" she asked. "You are just one man."

Moses pointed to the Midianites working outside their tent—in the fields, at the well. "Look at them. They have hopes and dreams. They have the promise of a life with dignity. That is what I want for my own people. That is why I must do the task God has given me."

"Then I will go with you," Tzipporah replied.

So, taking his wife, Moses—who was once a prince of Egypt and was now a simple shepherd—returned to the land of his birth.

In the many years since Moses had last been in Egypt, time had not stood still. New monuments had been raised up and new temples built, all by the hard labor of the Hebrew slaves. Moses scarcely recognized the buildings he had known as a boy, or the roads he had raced over as a young man.

Now Rameses ruled in his dead father's place. He was Egypt's morning and evening star. His word was the Egyptian law.

But the Hebrew slaves were not treated any better by Rameses than they had been by his father. If anything, they were worse off than ever before.

When Moses returned, Rameses was delighted. He would have pardoned forever any crime of which Moses stood accused.

"You are our brother, Moses," said Rameses. "You are a prince of Egypt."

Moses sighed. "In my heart you are my brother. But things cannot be as they were. You know I am Hebrew. The God of the Hebrews came to me and commanded that you let my people go."

"I do not know this God," Rameses said. "Neither will I let your people go."

Moses threw his shepherd's staff on the alabaster floor and called on the power of the Lord God. As everyone in the throne room watched, his staff turned into a great snake that twisted and writhed and flicked out its forked tongue, smiling a snake's smile, which is all fangs and no lips.

Rameses laughed and summoned his own magicians. "Show him that our gods, too, can play this game."

The magicians threw down their rods, which became snakes, too, slithering over the polished floor.

But in the shadows, Moses' great snake devoured the smaller snakes.

Then Moses bent down and picked up the great snake, which became a simple shepherd's staff once again.

But it was as if Pharaoh's heart had hardened with a sudden hatred. Taking Moses aside, Rameses said: "Tell your people that as of today their work shall be doubled." He gave the taskmasters leave to whip the slaves even more than before. Each lash Moses felt as if the sting were on his own back.

Still, the harsher treatment made the Hebrews turn against Moses, crying bitterly. "You have put a sword in his hand to kill us."

Even Aaron, his brother, cried out against him.

Moses fell down before their righteous anger.

Only Miriam stood up for him. "God saved you from the river. God saved you in your wanderings. God will not abandon you now. Do not abandon us."

As if Miriam's words were the Lord's words, Moses stood. He grasped his staff and went to the River Nile where the royal barge floated. Calling out in a voice made great by the power of God, he cried, "Rameses, let my people go."

Rameses scarcely turned his head. "Carry on," he commanded his sailors.

Moses called out again. "Let my people go."

This time the Pharaoh had had enough. "I will hear no more Hebrew nonsense," he said. Turning to the guards, he ordered, "Bring him to me."

So Moses took his staff and struck the water with the rod. At the blow, the Nile turned to blood. The canals turned to blood. The ponds turned to blood. Even the standing pools of water turned to blood. And the guards in the blood-filled Nile screamed out to their own gods for help.

But the Pharaoh's own magicians played a trick with a bowl of water, turning it from blue white to blood red and displayed it to Pharaoh. Their trick confirmed what the Pharaoh already believed, and he would not let the Hebrew people go.

Then Moses said to Pharaoh, "If you refuse to let the Hebrew people go, God will bring down upon you plague after plague after plague. Not just the turning of water into blood, but plagues of frogs and lice and flies. Cattle pestilence and boils. Thunder and hail, and scavenging locusts. There will be a plague of darkness all over the land."

But Pharaoh would not change his mind and the plagues began.

After each plague, Moses was certain that Pharaoh would relent.

But really his heart was becoming like a crust of old bread: dry and hard. Each time a plague was over, he would not let the Hebrew people go.

Then Moses came to Rameses one last time, no longer speaking like a brother. "No kingdom should be made on the backs of slaves," he said. "Your stubbornness is bringing this misery upon Egypt."

Rameses shook his head. "I will not be dictated to! I will not be threatened! I am the morning and the evening star. I am Pharaoh." He would not be moved.

So the Lord said to Moses and Moses told the Hebrew slaves that they should take a lamb and kill it. Then with a bunch of hyssop dipped in its blood, mark the lintel and posts of every door.

"For tonight," Moses said, "the Lord shall pass through the land of Egypt and smite all the firstborn. But where the Lord sees the blood upon the door, the Lord will pass over you and the plague shall not enter."

And so it was done.

Late that night, when death moved like mist, like fog, through all of Egypt, it passed over the houses marked with lamb's blood, but it came into the houses with unmarked doors. It entered the houses of potters and the houses of the palace guard. It entered the homes of wise men and the homes of fools.

And it entered the room where Pharaoh's own son lay sleeping.

Then a great cry went out all through Egypt, for there was not a house that was untouched, except for the houses of the Hebrews with the blood mark over the doors.

Pharaoh sent for Moses in the middle of the night, and when Moses arrived he saw Rameses standing over his son's body which was laid out on a great slab.

"You," Rameses said in a voice that was as dead as stone. "You and your people have my permission to go." His voice, like his heart, was hard. But his heart was harder still.

And Moses wept.

The Pharaoh's words spread through the slave quarters and when the Hebrew people heard that they were free, they cried out: "There can be miracles!"

Then, quickly, before the Pharaoh could change his mind, they gathered all that they owned. They moved so fast, they took their dough before it was leavened and bound their kneading troughs on their shoulders.

They took their flocks and their lambs, and what small treasures they had, and fled through the dark streets. Hundreds of men, women, and children.

Dawn found them hastening past the deserted work sites: thousands of men, women, and children.

Midday found them funneling through the desert valleys and into the wilderness: thousands upon thousands upon thousands.

Free.

Free at last.

They walked many days and came to the shores of the Red Sea.
There they rested and rejoiced greatly. But Egypt was not done with them yet.

Rameses, with his hard heart, had changed his mind.

He called for his soldiers. He sent for his six hundred war chariots. Then, at
the head of this vast army, he raced through the wilderness after his Hebrew slaves.

Cresting a hill, Rameses saw the great horde of Hebrews spread out along
the banks of the sea and he smiled. It was the serpent's smile.

The Hebrew people saw the Egyptian army and trembled. "Have you brought us here only to die, Moses?" they cried. "Were there not graves enough in Egypt?"

As if answering their cry, the Lord sent a pillar of fire to block the army. Then the Lord called out, "Lift up your staff, Moses."

So Moses lifted the staff and the Lord divided the Red Sea between two great transparent walls of water. On either side, little colored fish darted, great-bellied leviathan swam, and the many-armed jellyfish pulsed and eels slithered. But there was dry land between the walls.

The Hebrew people started across that rock-strewn path to the farther side.

Some walked, some stumbled, most ran.

When they were safely across, the pillar of fire disappeared. Like dogs let loose after a hare, the Egyptian soldiers bolted onto the rocky path between the transparent walls, eager for the kill.

When all but Rameses were in the center of the divided waters, the Lord let the walls close. The Red Sea gave a mighty roar and fell back into its accustomed place, drowning all the soldiers at once.

There was a sudden silence as deep and as profound as the sea. On opposite shores, two men stood silently, mourning for what lay under that sea. Moses for the loss of his childhood. And Rameses for the might that had been Egypt and the glory that had once been his own.

But their thoughts were suddenly shattered by a mighty shout.

"There can be miracles!" cried the Hebrew people. "Now we are truly free."

And the people sang and danced on the shore, they played on harps and timbrels, so great was their joy.

Then Moses joined them. Where once he had made their pain his pain, now he made their joy his joy.

The Hebrew people wandered in the desert for three full moons.

At last Moses led them to the foot of Mount Sinai. There, at the Lord's bidding, he climbed up to the mountaintop to receive two tablets of stone on which the Lord's ten commandments—the laws for living a moral life—were carved.

As Moses stood looking down at the people below, his own people, he recalled that he had once been a prince of Egypt, serving at the whim of the Pharaoh. He had lived in a land where the many served the few. But now, standing on Mount Sinai with the Lord's tablets in his arms, he knew that he was serving something far greater—the One God.

He lifted the tablets so that everyone could see as he came down the rocky path.

And the people rejoiced greatly.